5-Minute Daily Practice

Vocabulary

BY KATHLEEN FITZGIBBON

SCHOLASTIC
PROFESSIONAL BOOKS

New York • Toronto • London • Auckland • Sydney • Mexico City
New Delhi • Hong Kong • Buenos Aires

A special thanks to Sarah Glasscock,
Virginia Dooley, and Maria Chang for giving me this opportunity.

Scholastic Inc. grants teachers permission to photocopy the reproducible pages for classroom use. No other part of
this publication may be reproduced in whole or in part, or stored in a retrieval system, or transmitted in any form or by any
means, electronic, mechanical, photocopying, recording, or otherwise, without written permission of the publisher.
For information regarding permission, write to Scholastic Inc.,557 Broadway, New York, NY 10012.

Cover design by **Gerard Fuchs**
Cover art by **Dave Clegg**
Interior design by **Holly Grundon**
Interior illustrations by **Mike Moran, Teresa Anderko, and Kate Flanagan**

ISBN: 0-439-46607-5
Copyright © 2003 by Kathleen Fitzgibbon
All rights reserved. Published by Scholastic Inc.
Printed in the U.S.A.

5 6 7 8 9 10   40   09 08 07 06

5-Minute Daily Practice

Contents

Introduction

We've all seen students get bogged down in their reading when they encounter unfamiliar words. Vocabulary development is not only key to improving reading comprehension, it also helps students with both writing and speaking. And it carries over to all other content areas, too. But how can you fit vocabulary instruction into your already full days?

With one simple, five-minute exercise each day, you can reinforce your students' vocabulary skills. The 180 activities in this book are designed to make teaching vocabulary quick, easy, and fun. They are organized into eight sections. These sections include the most common techniques for learning new words: context clues and etymology; understanding the meanings of prefixes; understanding the meanings of suffixes; understanding the meanings of Latin and Greek roots; synonyms; antonyms; and homophones and homonyms. In addition, a section of word games provides fun and challenging ways for students to boost their vocabularies.

Classroom Management

This book is designed for flexible use. You may want to copy each page, cut apart the activities, and post one on a bulletin board each day. You may prefer to copy them onto the blackboard. Another alternative is to make an overhead transparency of each page. Leave all but the daily activity covered each day. Here are some other ways to use these activities.

How to Use These Activities

Most of the activities in *5-Minute Daily Practice: Vocabulary* are intended for independent work. Copy the activities onto index cards and let students choose a card. Students can use reference materials such as dictionaries or thesauruses, or they can just use their own imaginations to complete activities designed to enhance their vocabularies.

Many games and activities in *5-Minute Daily Practice: Vocabulary* are designed for work with a partner. Students compete, cooperate, and collaborate in these activities. The activities designed for individual work can also be done cooperatively with a partner.

The activities in the Word Games section can easily be played in either small or large groups. When you want to involve many students, choose one of these activities and allow students to bounce ideas off one another, work as a team, or delegate tasks.

Integrate Activities With Your Curriculum

Have students work through the activities in *5-Minute Daily Practice: Vocabulary* using words from the vocabulary list you are currently studying. Many activities are open-ended for flexibility. You can choose specific activities from one section to reinforce your lessons. For example, if you are studying prefixes, choose the appropriate activities from the Prefixes section for independent student work.

Engage Your Students

Each activity in *5-Minute Daily Practice: Vocabulary* is designed to stand alone. They are not presented in any particular order within each section. Choose activities based on skill or student appeal. Let your students have fun with the activities in *5-Minute Daily Practice: Vocabulary*. Use them to enrich your classroom instruction and contribute to your goal of creating a classroom in which a love of words and a love of reading is nurtured.

Name: _____

1. Do you speak French? Define and use *etiquette, memoir, corps, coup,* and *encore* in sentences. You've just added five French/English words to your vocabulary!

I had a chocolate mousse at the café on the boulevard.

Name: _____

2. Choose a vocabulary word that is a noun. Write a poem made up of clues describing your noun, but don't use the noun in the poem. Exchange poems with a classmate and try to guess which noun is the poem's subject.

Example:
It's your first day.
You are brand-new.
You'll know your way,
In a week—or two.
—novice

Name: _____

3. How would you solve each problem?

A   Your computer ceases.

B   Your dog and cat won't bond.

C   There is not a remnant of cake left.

D   Your tent collapses.

Name: _____

4. Complete the analogy! Figure out the relationship of the first pair of words and then complete the second pair, which will be related in the same way.

One is to two as sixty-four is to _____ .

Evening is to night as August is to _____ .

Cow is to herd as bird is to _____ .

Mitt is to catcher as whistle is to _____ .

Now make up an analogy of your own!

Name: _____

5. English is full of words borrowed from other languages. Etymology is the study of word histories. What's the etymology of *patio, plaza, llama, coyote,* and *junta*? Use each in a sentence.

Name: _____

6. Write an answering machine message using as many of your vocabulary words as you can.

Name: _____

7. Think of something you'd like to sell (it can be real or made up). Write an ad for a newspaper describing what you're selling. Include as many vocabulary words as you can!

Example:
One defective calculator for sale. Suitable for people who do not want to balance their checkbooks! Payment in cash only! A mere $25.

Name: _____

8. A concrete poem shows all! Write a poem that shows the meaning of a word in both the text and the shape of the poem.

Boomerang.

No matter how many times

You give away this poem,

It keeps coming back.

Boomerang. No matter how many times you give away this poem, it keeps coming back.

Name: _____

9. Pick a word that has many meanings. Write the word in a box in the middle of your paper. Write as many sentences as you can that use each different meaning of the word. Connect the sentences to the box in the middle.

This year's fair had the best rides ever.

It wasn't fair that Alexa got a head start.

Nick has fair hair and freckles.

fair

I hope we have fair weather tomorrow.

Context Clues and Etymology

Name: _____

10. Use *foundation*, *install*, *structure*, and *derrick* in a paragraph about the construction of a building.

Context Clues and Etymology

Name: _____

11. It's time for the curtain to go up! Illustrate each of these theater words:

scenery   audience   wardrobe   balcony   spotlight

Context Clues and Etymology

Name: _____

12. With a partner, pick a pair of your favorite characters. They could be Batman and Robin, Michael Jordan and Scotty Pippen, or Snow White and Sleepy. Write a dialogue between the two characters using your vocabulary words in the conversation.

Name: _____

13. A Tom Swifty is a sentence ending in an adverb that tells both how or when Tom said something. The adverb has to do with what Tom said. For example:

"Here comes a fire truck," yelled Tom alarmingly.

"I missed the train," cried Tom belatedly.

"Who took the modern art painting?" asked Tom abstractedly.

Now write three Tom Swifties.

Name: _____

14. Feelings, feelings, feelings . . . . Each of the words describes a feeling. For each word, draw a picture (stick figures will do) and a speech bubble that express the feelings.

　　　　sympathetic　　　　wistful　　　　confused　　　　elated

Name: _____

15. What would you do with . . .

Leisure time?

Too many assignments?

A deflated tire?

A multitude of quarters?

A dinner of foods that you loathe?

Context Clues and Etymology

Name: _____

16. Picture dictionaries are not just for little kids! Make a picture dictionary of nouns. Draw a picture for each word or cut one from a magazine or catalog. Add to your dictionary as you come across new nouns. Try starting with train words, such as *boxcar*, *gondola*, *caboose*, and *Pullman*.

Context Clues and Etymology

Name: _____

17. What's that? An animal parade? Match each of these movement words to an animal that might move that way:

plod	dart	flit	lope	meander
skim	gallop	slither	slink	lumber

Context Clues and Etymology

Name: _____

18. Write the letters *m–i–r–t–h* vertically on a sheet of paper. Use each letter as the first letter of words that make you joyful. Then write a definition for the word *mirth*.

Example:

M u s i c

I _____

R _____

T _____

H _____

Name: _____

19. Have you ever worn a blouse, dungarees, a pinafore, galoshes, or a chapeau? Illustrate and label each with a sentence. You might want to use a dictionary or a fashion magazine to help you.

Name: _____

20. You just got a job as the food reviewer for the local paper. You go to the first restaurant and the food is boring! Write a review using *bland*, *flavorless*, *mediocre*, and *drab* in it.

Name: _____

21. Try these:

1. Put the numbers 12, 13, 14, 15, 16, 17, and 18 in haphazard order.

2. Draw a picture of a labyrinth.

3. List the clothes you would pack to visit a sultry climate.

Name: _____

22. Pull a nonfiction book off the shelf. Use sticky notes to label the following parts of the book:

spine   publisher   copyright   preface   glossary   folio

Name: _____

23. Draw a cartoon character or stick figure doing each of the following:

collapsing   contracting   slouching   vaulting

Name: _____

24. Make your face sneer, scowl, stare, glare, wince, and squint. Get a partner to guess each expression you make.

Name: _____

25. Use each of the words below in a sentence. Then use the plural form of each in a sentence. Yes, it's tricky! A dictionary will help you.

salmon   index   radius

focus   parenthesis   medium

Name: _____

26. Answer these questions:

What does a lobbyist do?

Have you ever met a radiologist? What did that person do?

How would a chauffeur make your life easier?

How does a benefactor help others?

Name: _____

27. Write a description of an eminent person. Use the words *utmost*, *peerless*, *outstanding*, and *notable* in your paragraph.

Name: _____

28. Do you think you're a comedian? Use these words in a paragraph or two about something funny:

comedian   facetious   prank   whimsical   hilarious

Name: _____

29. Have you had a bad day? Write about it. Be sure to include these words in your piece:

bemoan   whimper   whine   lament   grumble

Name: _____

30. Words that are borrowed from people's names are called eponyms. For example, *maverick* came from Samuel Maverick, a Texas rancher who refused to brand his cattle. Read these stories and figure out what word was borrowed from each person's name:

1. In 1871, students at Yale University played catch with pie tins from William Frisbe's pie company.

2. Ambrose Burnside was the governor of Rhode Island and a general during the Civil War. He wore thick whiskers on the sides of his face.

3. During the Crimean War, the Earl of Cardigan had his soldiers knit sweaters.

4. Anton Sax combined a clarinet's reed with oboe fingering and developed a musical instrument.

Name: _____

31. Look through a dictionary to find an unfamiliar word. Write a few sentences using the new word and including clues to the word's meaning. Exchange papers with classmates and try to figure out the meaning of their new words.

Example:
Even though the fire was burning up the forest, the phlegmatic man sat calmly. Nothing worried him. He watched the approaching flames and slowly lifted the water hose and turned the water on.

Name: _____

32. Do you speak Spanish? Define and use *corral, lasso, rodeo, bonanza,* and *yucca* in sentences. You've just added five Spanish/English words to your vocabulary!

Name: _____

33. Make a noun diagram. Draw a picture and label each part with the following flight words: *fuselage, cockpit, cargo,* and *propeller.*

Context Clues and Etymology 5-Minute Daily Practice

Name: _____

34. Choose from the words below to write a description of a pleasant person. Use the remaining words to describe an unpleasant person.

arrogant   considerate   cooperative   cordial

disrespectful   brusque   generous   rude

Name: _____

35. Lots of people mix up the words below. Let's get them straight once and for all! Use each word in a sentence that makes its meaning clear.

accept   except   expect

moral   morale   mortal

Name: _____

36. What topic is someone writing about if they use the words *volume, audio, tempo, harmony,* and *vocalist*? Write a paragraph on that topic. Include each of the five words in it.

Name: ....

37. Have you ever confused some words just because their spellings are similar? Use each of these words in a sentence that makes its meaning clear.

dessert, desert

advise, advice

latter, later

breathe, breath

Name: ....

38. Try writing your own comic strip. Cut out a comic strip from the newspaper. Cover the text in the speech bubble. Now write your own dialogue in the bubbles using as many vocabulary words as you can.

Name: ....

39. Write a short story about spending time at the mall. Include the words *currency*, *merchant*, *markup*, and *stock* in your story.

Name: _____

40. Be prepared! Explain what clothing or other special equipment you'll need for each day's weather:

Monday	Tuesday	Wednesday	Thursday	Friday
blizzard	drizzle	cyclone	heat wave	sleet

Name: _____

41. Draw a building layout and label the following:

foyer   boudoir   threshold   vestibule   portico   pantry

Name: _____

42. Did you ever stumble over an unfamiliar word while reading? Find an unfamiliar word and copy the sentence you found it in on a sheet of paper. Look up the meaning of the word and write down its definition. Then rewrite the sentence using a synonym or phrase to replace the unfamiliar word.

Name: _____

43. Write a paragraph about a visit to the library. You may write about a personal experience or make up a silly story. Be sure to include the words *encyclopedia*, *literature*, *classic*, *fable*, and *narrative* in your story.

Name: _____

44. How's your Italian? Define and use the words *viola*, *bravo*, *tempo*, *piccolo*, *gusto*, and *gondola* in sentences. You've just added six Italian/English words to your vocabulary!

Name: _____

45. What is a . . .

divan   settee   ottoman   wardrobe   credenza   recliner

Illustrate each. In what store would you buy them?

Name: _____

46. When the U.S. bought Alaska from Russia, new words came into American English. Define and illustrate *igloo, mukluk,* and *parka.*

Name: _____

47. Look up *pre-* in the dictionary. Pick two words that start with *pre-*. Write riddles that define these words. Did you use *before* in your definitions? You should!

Name: _____

48. Write one word with the prefix that means *one*. (That's *mono-* or *uni-*.) Write two words with the prefix that means *two*. Write three words with the prefix that means *three*. Then really challenge yourself: How many words can you find that begin with the prefix that means *four*? How about *five*?

Prefixes

Name: _____

49. Make *un-* Positive/Negative Dictionaries. Start by stapling five pieces of paper together to form a ten-page book. On the front of each page, write a word with the prefix *un-*. On the back of each page, write the base or root word upside down. Write a dictionary entry under each word. When you read the book one way, you find only positive words. When you flip the book over and read it the other way, you get negative words.

Prefixes

Name: _____

50. Pick three of these words:

biography   autobiography   biology   biodegradable   biopsy   bionic

Write a definition for each. Now do you know what the prefix *bio-* means?

Prefixes

Name: _____

51. Pick three of these words:

superhuman   supernova   superpower   supernatural   superstar

Write a definition for each. Now do you know what the prefix *super-* means?

Prefixes

Name: _____

52. What do the prefixes *in-*, *un-*, and *ir-* have in common? Define *inactive*, *unable*, and *irresponsible*. What word did you use in each definition? I'm not going to give you any clues!

Prefixes

Name: _____

53. Define *indifferent*, *incomparable*, and *inadequate* with words that start with *un-*.

Prefixes

Name: _____

54. If the prefix *circum-* means *around*, how would you define *circumscribe*, *circuit*, *circumference*, and *circumnavigate*?

Name: _____

55. Look up the definitions for the words *automatic*, *automobile*, and *autograph*. Now see if you can figure out what the Greek word *auto* means.

Name: _____

56. Dive into this one! List as many words as you can that have the prefix *aqua-*. Compare lists with a partner. What could *aqua-* possibly mean?

Name: _____

57. What prefixes are in each of these words?

precise   concise   incision   decisive

Define each word. (Hint: *cis* means *to cut or kill.*)

Name: _____

58. Try these word transformers, writing down the new word you make at each step:

1. Put the prefix *in-* onto verse.
2. Add the suffix *-ion*.
3. Change the *in-* prefix to *con-*.

1. Put the prefix *sub-* onto vert.
2. Change the *sub-* prefix to *extro-*.
3. Change the *extro-* prefix to *intro-* to make a word that means the opposite of the last word you made.

Pick and define three of the words you made.
Do you have any idea what *verse/vert* means?

Name: _____

59. What prefix is missing? (Hint: It means *far off*.)

_____ vision   _____ phone   _____ graph   _____ scope

This one is harder. What prefix is missing? (Hint: It means *over*, *across*, or *beyond*. Need another hint? It begins with the same letter as the first prefix in this activity.)

_____ form   _____ late   _____ port   _____ parent

Name: _____

60. *Meter* comes from the Greek word for measure. What are you measuring with each of these words?

thermometer   centimeter   diameter   barometer

1 2 3 4 5 6 7 8 9 10 11 12

Name: _____

61. *Hemi-* and *semi-* both mean *half*. Name one word for each prefix and write a dictionary definition for both words. Include an example sentence in each definition. Did you use *half* in each definition? You should!

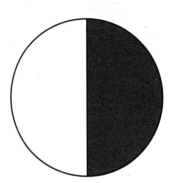

Name: _____

62. If the prefix *mis-* means *bad,* what do *misbehave, misconduct,* and *misfortune* mean? Use each in a sentence.

Name: _____

63. Use the prefix in each to help you list the antonym for each of these words.

disagree   disarm   discontinue   dishonest

Write pairs of sentences that show the opposite meanings.

Example:
I am dissatisfied with the awful stew I made.
I am satisfied with the delicious stew I made.

Name: ....

64. It's how big? The prefixes *magni-*, *mega-*, and *micro-* describe size.
Use words with some or all of those prefixes to describe something large.
Use words with some or all of those prefixes to describe something small.

Name: ....

65. Define *preamble*, *prefix*, and *prologue* with definitions that explain when those things took place.

Name: ....

66. With a partner, pick two of these words:

coauthor   coincide   cooperate   coordinate

Write a definition for each. Now do you know what the prefix *co-* means? Find another *co-* word to add to the list.

Name: _____

67. What is the prefix and root word in the word review? Add new prefixes to the root word to make up four of your own new words. They can be real or make-believe words, but be sure to provide a definition for each word.

Example:
disview—ignore or fail to see

Name: _____

68. Add the prefix *sub-* to *floor, way, base, freezing, normal,* and *marine.* Use the meanings of those words to figure out the meaning of the prefix *sub-*. Add another *sub-* word to the list.

Name: _____

69. When did the following take place?

postgraduate   posthumous   postmortem   postscript   postwar

Can you figure out what the prefix *post-* means?

Name: ....

70. What Latin root is found in the words *reform*, *perform*, *inform*, *conform*, and *transform*? What prefixes were added to the Latin root? Using what you know about those prefixes, define two of the words.

Name: ....

71. Sketch a picture of a *telescope*, *microscope*, *stethoscope*, and a *periscope*. What would you see with each?

Name: ....

72. List four words with the prefix *ab-*. The prefix *ab-* means *away from*. Define each word using *away from* in each definition.

> Example:
>
> abnormal—away from normal

Prefixes

Name: _____

73. Try this word transformer, writing down the new word you make at each step:

1. Add the prefix *trans-* to port.   _____

2. Add the suffix *-ation* to the word you just made.   _____

3. Change the prefix to *de-*.   _____

4. Drop the suffix.   _____

5. Change the prefix to *pro-* and add the suffix *–ion*.   _____

Use a dictionary to define the five words you made.

Prefixes

Name: _____

74. If the prefix *ex-* means *out*, what do the words *exit*, *exhale*, *exceed*, *exclaim*, and *expand* mean?

Prefixes

Name: _____

75. Dig through a dictionary to make a list of words with the prefix *col-*. Make sure each word in your list has *together* somewhere in the definition. *Colony* will work but *collar* will not!

Name: _____

76. Define *contraband*, *contradict*, and *contrast*. What prefix do all three words share? What does it mean? Can't figure it out? Find a partner. And put your heads together to see if you can define it.

Name: _____

77. Start with the word *active*. Add suffixes and/or prefixes to change *active* into different parts of speech. How many new words did you make?

"What activity is this?"

Name: _____

78. Do you know what suffix means *to do* or *to make*? It's the common suffix *–ize*. List five real and made-up words that have the suffix *–ize*. Exchange lists with a classmate and write a definition for each word that includes the base or root word.

Example: apologize, summarize, fertilize, porkchopize, sketchize

Name: _____

79. What do the words *motionless, thoughtless, toothless, nameless,* and *hopeless* have in common? Write a definition for each word that includes its base or root word. Can you write a definition for the suffix *–less*?

Name: _____

80. What are the root words of

feverish   selfish   devilish   childish   Swedish

Can you figure out what the suffix *–ish* means?
Add it to three words to describe yourself.

Name: _____

81. Don't be shy . . . define *intimidate.*
What's its root word? Define the root
word. Add a new suffix to the root
word. Define the new word. How are
all the definitions related?

Name: _____

82. Work carefully through this activity. Many adverbs end in *-ly*.
List four actions you do outdoors. Then match an *-ly* adverb
to each and write a sentence using the word pairs you formed.
Example: jump happily

Name: _____

83. Yes, there is such a word as *antidisestablishmentarianism*.
It means *the state support of a church*. This word has
many suffixes and prefixes. List all the prefixes and all
the suffixes. Then write a more common word using
each prefix and suffix.

Name: _____

84. The suffixes *–ian* and *-arian* mean *a person who is, or who does*. Add one
of these suffixes to each of the words below. (Hint: You might need to
adjust a word's spelling before adding the suffix.) Then use each new word
in a sentence.

clinic   diet   library   humanity   Italy

Name: _____

85. If you want to form nouns from adjectives ending in *–ile, –il, -able,* or *–ible,* add the suffix *–ility. Capability* is a noun formed from the adjective *capable.* Make nouns from the adjectives *agile* and *durable.* Now come up with three of your own.

Name: _____

86. What words mean *full of wonder, full of fear, full of care,* and *full of beauty*? (Hint: The suffix *–ful* means *full of.*) Write definitions for four more *–ful* words. Give them to a partner to figure out which words you defined.

87. Imagine that you own your own car. Write a description of your vehicle using as many adjectives as you can that have the suffix *–er* or *-est.*

(Hint: To compare two things, use *–er.* To compare three or more things, use *–est.*)

Name: _____

88. What are you doing if you are:

Shopping impulsively?

Eating ravenously?

Laughing wholeheartedly?

Name: _____

89. The suffix –*ly* is used at the end of many adverbs.
Carefully use –*ly* adverbs to complete this activity.

1. How did it move?

2. When did it happen?

3. How did it happen?

Use your adverbs to write a short, short story about "it."

Name: _____

90. The suffix -*ment* can mean the *state or quality of*. Find the base words in *settlement, arrangement, advertisement, entertainment*, and *announcement*. Use the suffix meaning as you write a definition for each word.

Name: _____

91. The suffix *–uous* means *state or quality of.* Add the suffix to each of the words below and use each new word in a sentence. (Hint: You might need to adjust the spelling before adding the suffix.)

continue   mystery   contempt   vary

Name: _____

92. Ever seen a caricature? It's a drawing that tells about a person by exaggerating his or her features, clothing, or tools. The noun suffix *–or* means *one who.* For example an actor is *one who acts.* List three *–or* nouns, then draw a caricature for each.

Name: _____

93. What are the root words of *adjustment, engagement, contentment,* and *establishment?* Define those root words.

Name: _____

94. Can it Be Done? Use the six words below in an advertisement for an imaginary product. You may need to use a dictionary to help you!

"This is impossible!"

possible	invisible	permissible
combustible	horrible	edible

Name: _____

95. Psyche has to do with the mind. Use what you know about suffixes to define *psychology*, *psychotic*, *psychopath*, and *psychosomatic*.

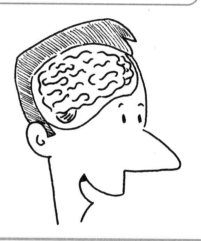

Name: _____

96. Don't be afraid of this activity! The Greek word *phobos* means "fear." Have you heard of *claustrophobia*? It's a fear of closed spaces. How about *aquaphobia*? It's a fear of water. Make up and define a list of phobias. You might want to use these Greek root words or other roots you know.

aero = air	dont = tooth	opt = eye	photo = light
andr = man	geo = earth	ped = child	therm = heat
dem = people	neo = new	phon = sound	poli = city

Name: _____

97. The Latin root *cide* means *killing*. Define the following *cide* words using the word killing in each definition.

insecticide   pesticide   bactericide

herbicide   homicide   suicide

Name: _____

98. The Latin root *neg* means *not*. A negative answer means that you said *no*. Find three words with *neg* and define each using a negative word in each definition.

Name: _____

99. The suffix *-ject* means *to throw*. Use what you know about each of the prefixes to define these four words: *deject*, *object*, *inject*, and *subject*.

Name: _____

100. Add the prefixes *tele-*, *dia-*, *epi-*, and *mono-* to the Greek root *gram*. Write a definition for each word. (Hint: *Gram* means *letter, written*.)

Name: _____

101. What prefixes were added to the Greek root *graph* to form *telegraph*, *photograph*, *phonograph*, and *autograph*? What does *graph* mean? Write a definition for each word that includes the meaning of *graph* in the definition.

Name: _____

102. The Latin root *port* means "to carry." Write a definition for *transport*, *support*, *import*, *export*, and *deport*. Can you include *to carry* in each definition?

Latin and Greek Roots

Name: _____

103. Have you ever noticed the root *tain*? It's another root from Latin and it means *to hold*. Define *retain*, *contain*, *detain*, and *attain*, keeping in mind the meaning of the prefix plus the Latin root as you write each definition.

Latin and Greek Roots

Name: _____

104. Construct sentences for these words with the Latin root struct:

structure   instruct

destruct   construct

Latin and Greek Roots

Name: _____

105. What comes out of a hydrant?

What kind of treatment are you getting in hydrotherapy?

What do you need if you are dehydrated?

Where does hydroelectric power come from?

Using your answers, define the Greek word *hydr*.

Name: _____

106. Vitality comes from the Latin word *vita*. *Vita* means *life*. Find three words that come from *vita*. Make sure that the definition of each has something to do with *life*.

Name: _____

107. *Spectacle, spectacular, spectator,* and *spectroscope* all come from the Latin word *spectare,* which means *to behold*. How do the definitions for each of these words relate to that old Latin word?

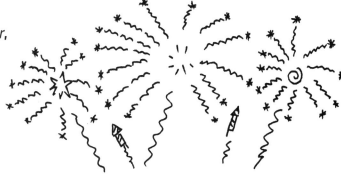

Name: _____

108. You don't need to speak Greek! *Thermometer, thermal, thermostat,* and *thermos* all have the Greek root *therm*. Using the definition of each of these words, see if you can figure out the meaning of *therm*.

5-Minute Daily Practice

Name: _____

109. If you know that the Greek root *aud* means *hear*, it can help you define words containing *aud*. List five words that come from the root *aud* and define them. Get your list started with *audience*.

"We can't hear you!"

Name: _____

110. What three-letter root that means *make, do* is found in the words: *factor*, *manufacture*, *benefactor*, and *facsimile*? Find the definition of each word. Tell a partner or write down how each word has something to do with *make* or *do*.

Name: _____

111. The Latin root *ped* means *foot*. What does a foot have to do with the meaning of *pedal*, *pedestrian*, *biped*, and *pedestal*?

Name: _____

112. The little Latin root *vac* means *empty*. Define *vacant, vacation, vacuum,* and *vacate*. What does *empty* have to do with each of those words?

Name: _____

113. Use a thesaurus to find five synonyms for *angry*. Then write a dialogue between two people using your five new words.

Name: _____

114. You have three minutes to list all the words you can that describe love or affection. After you've made your list, pick your three favorites and use each in a sentence. Now . . . go!

Name: _____

115. Complete the analogy! The first one is done as an example.

Draw is to __illustrate__ as laugh is to giggle.

Astonish is to _____ as allow is to let.

Fragile is to _____ as happy is to glad.

Accelerate is to _____ as like is to enjoy.

Occur is to _____ as say is to state.

Slender is to _____ as fat is to chubby.

Numerous is to _____ as right is to correct.

Name: _____

116. Copy a sentence from a story you like. Underline one word in the sentence and then replace that word with a synonym. Explain how it changed the meaning of the sentence.

Name: _____

117. What color is that? Is it teal? Olive? Beige? Sepia? Chartreuse? Burgundy? Mauve? Taupe? Find and list a synonym for each of these color words. When you come across other unusual color words, add them to your list.

Name: _____

118. Did you ever hear the proverb "You can't infuse an elderly canine contemporary stunts"? That's a funny way of saying "You can't teach an old dog new tricks." Translate these common proverbs into their more common forms (you might want to have a thesaurus handy):

The vegetation constantly appears more viridescent on the variant side.

The premature fowl grasps the worm.

Name: _____

119. You have three minutes to list all the words you can that describe sadness. After you've made your list, pick your three favorites and use them in a paragraph. Now . . . go!

Name: _____

120. There are so many other words to use besides *said*. List verbs that show the speaker is excited. List verbs that show the speaker is talking softly. List verbs that show the speaker is whining. List verbs that show the speaker is sad.

Name: _____

121. Have a Thesaurus Scavenger Hunt by following these steps:

1. List four synonyms for the noun *bag*.

2. Replace the underlined word in this sentence with a synonym.

3. Find two synonyms for *pretty*. Use each in a sentence.

4. How did you do? List two synonyms for *perfect*.

Name: _____

122. Find and list synonyms for *small*. Write a story about what happened to you when you woke one morning and found that you were only six inches tall. Use as many of your small synonyms as you can.

Synonyms

Name: _____

123. Bon Voyage! It's time to take a trip. List synonyms for *journey*. Write a story about a trip using as many synonyms from your list as you can.

Example:
When the cruise ship docked in the port, I was the first one off the ship. I soon met a tour guide.

Synonyms

Name: _____

124. Terminate! Cease! Pause! Discontinue! Halt! Stop what you're doing and use each of those synonyms in place of *stop* in a sentence.

Synonyms

Name: _____

125. Find all the synonyms you can for *illness*. Pick your favorite four and use them in a short story.

Synonyms

Name: _____

126. You have three minutes to list all the words you can that describe *joy* or *elation*. After you've made your list, pick your three favorites and illustrate each. Now . . . go!

Synonyms

Name: _____

127. Write a synonym for each adverb. Write a complete sentence for each of your new adverbs that includes the verb the adverb is modifying.

rapidly   cleverly   frequently   tidily   brilliantly

Example:
The dog ran swiftly to his bowl.

Synonyms

Name: _____

128. You have three minutes to list all the words you can that describe *fear* or *anxiety*. After you've made your list, pick your three favorites and use them in a description of something scary. Now . . . go!

Name: _____

129. List synonyms for anyone younger than you. Start with *child* and *youngster*. Come on, you can come up with more than that! Use words from your list in a paragraph or two.

Name: _____

130. What do you want to be when you grow up? As you write your answer to this question, use as many synonyms as you can for the word *grow*.

Name: _____

131. List synonyms for *swell*. Now list an antonym for each word on your list.

Name: _____

132. Why use a big word when a simple one will do? Find a simpler synonym for each word listed below.

multitudinous   mortification   pandemonium   designation

competent   interrogate   sustenance   sufficient

Name: _____

133. This sign was posted in a cafeteria. Please rewrite it so everyone can understand it.

Will all of the sphere hurlers please be considerate and cease flinging orbs adjacent to edifices? Broken windows are a problem!

Name: _____

134. Sports writers often use very colorful, descriptive words. Look through the sports section of a newspaper and make a list of ten adjectives (words that describe something). On your own or using a thesaurus, list a synonym for each adjective you found.

Name: _____

135. How are the meanings of *excited*, *eager*, and *anxious* different? Use each in sentence that shows their meanings.

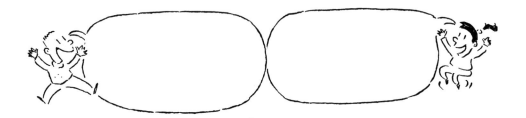

Name: _____

136. Complete the analogy! The first one is done as an example.

Hot is to <u>cold</u> as win is to lose.

Command is to _____ as back is to front.

Handsome is to _____ as big is to little.

Powerful is to _____ as hard is to soft.

Tragic is to _____ as sad is to happy.

Reduce is to _____ as gain is to lose.

Prohibit is to _____ as slow is to fast.

Name: _____

137. Write a pair of sentences that are the same except for one word, like the ones below. The words that are different should be antonyms. Write five more sentence pairs with a partner.

The innocent prisoner cried, "I didn't do it!"

The guilty prisoner cried, "I didn't do it!"

Name: _____

138. Copy a sentence from a story you like. Underline one word in the sentence. Now, replace that word with its antonym. Explain how it changed the meaning of the sentence.

Name: _____

139. You might not know the words below, but you probably know their antonyms. List each word and its antonym. Using a dictionary or thesaurus may help you.

carnivore   deciduous   arid   absorb   similar

Name: _____

140. Write a description of your *typical* school-day morning. Now write a description of an *atypical* morning.

Name: _____

141. List an antonym for each word below. Then try to use each pair of words in a sentence.

Word	antonym	Sentence
cackle		
guffaw		
snivel		
chortle		

Name: _____

142. Write a description of your greatest accomplishment. Now write a description of a failure.

Name: _____

143. Write a dialogue between a *pessimistic* and an *optimistic* person talking at a sporting event.

Antonyms

Name: _____

144. Name something in a kitchen that is opaque.

Name something that is transparent.

Name something you do in a kitchen preceding a meal.

Name something you do following a meal.

Antonyms

Name: _____

145. Write a factual statement. Write a fictitious statement. Write a commanding statement. Write an obeying statement.

Antonyms

Name: _____

146. What habit might a person want to maintain? What habit might a person want to discontinue? What at school do you find complex? What at school do you find simple?

$$4x - 3y = 24$$

Name: _____

147. What do the opposites *mobile* and *immobile* mean? Name a mobile object. Name an immobile object. *Mobile* comes from the Latin root *mobilis*. What could that Latin root mean? Now do you know what the prefix *im-* means?

Name: _____

148. Choose four words from this list:

achieve	add	answer	before	brave	continue	divide
help	hurry	keep	kind	make	mistake	noise
pain	praise	prohibit	shame	thaw	timid	vacant

Write down an antonym and synonym pair for each word you chose—but don't write down that word! Exchange your pairs with a partner. What words from the list match the pairs your partner wrote down?

Name: _____

149. Think about *chilly/chili, principal/principle, rumor/roomer* or even *you/yew/ewe!* Choose your own pair of homophones and write one sentence that includes both of them. Draw a picture to illustrate your sentence.

Name: _____

150. Homonyms are words that are spelled the same but have different meanings. Pick one of the homonyms below:

face   tire   stable   rare   pitcher

Write as many different meanings as you can for the word you chose. Compare your list with a partner. Then check to see if you matched the number in a dictionary.

Name: _____

151. Bob put a bob on the end of the fishing line and watched it bob up and down. That's three meanings for *bob*! Now try this:

Write two meanings for *passage*.   Write two meanings for *hamper*.

Write four meanings for *fair*.   Write two meanings for *maroon*.

Challenge yourself to use all the meanings for one of these words in one sentence.

Name: _____

152. Do you know of any words that are spelled the same but pronounced differently and have different meanings? Here's an example: The wind blew the shutters up just as I started to wind the clock. *Wind* and *wind* are homonyms. Find the different meanings for each homonym below. Then use each in a sentence.

minute   record   wound   contest

Name: _____

153. Form a team with one or two partners. Set a timer for four minutes. Each team lists as many homonyms as they can. Compare lists to see which team thought of the most.

Name: _____

154. Look for a word that sounds like *bow*, as in "tied the ribbon in a bow," but means "a man who is dating a woman."

Look for a word that sounds like *faze* but means "any stage in a series of changes."

Now make up your own clue for a classmate to find a word.

Name: _____

155. Look up each of the words below in a dictionary. Write the part or parts of speech for each word. Pick three of your favorites and write a sentence using each word as different parts of speech.

minor   mushroom   pinch   flash

Name: _____

156. Homonyms are words that are spelled the same but have different meanings. Pick one of the homonyms below:

lumber	colon	bay	bank	bound

Write as many different meanings as you can for the word you chose. Compare your list with a partner. Then check to see if you matched the number of meanings listed in a dictionary.

Name: _____

157. Correct the signs below. There are a total of seven mistakes.

One Our Parking Only	Sunrise Beech– Swimming Aloud	Smoking Band from the Area	Rough Rode Ahead	Write Tern

---

Name: _____

158. Write your vocabulary word vertically on paper. Use each letter as the first letter of a new word that relates to the vocabulary word. Yes, you can use a dictionary!

Example:

Q uiver
U rgent
A valanche
K nock
E mergency

Name: _____

159. It's Hink Pink time! Make up a question that is answered by two words that rhyme. The answer must include one of your vocabulary words.

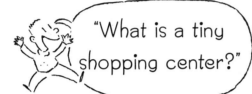 "What is a tiny shopping center?" "A small mall."

Name: _____

160. Ever see a diamond poem? Just follow these steps to write one:

Line 1: Write your vocabulary word.

Line 2: Write two words to describe your vocabulary word.

Line 3: Write three action words about it.

Line 4: Write a four- or five-word phrase describing the subject (not a complete sentence).

Line 5: Write a synonym for your vocabulary word.

You've just written a diamond poem!

Name: _____

161. Pull apart *antiferromagnetic*. Start by writing it on a sheet of paper. Find and list each prefix and suffix. Write a new word that contains each prefix and a new word that contains each suffix. Then write your own long word on a sheet of paper and challenge a classmate to pull it apart.

Name: _____

162. Play Answers and Questions! Make up an answer that describes each of your vocabulary words. Tell the answers to classmates and have them respond in the form of a question.

"This word names someone you might want if you needed help with math."

"What is a tutor?"

Name: _____

163. You're going on a trip. What would you pack for a vacation to the *tundra*? to a *summit*? to a *plateau*? to a *glacier*?

Name: _____

164. Play "How would you feel if . . . ?" by answering these questions. How would you feel if you ate abundant amounts of candy? How would you feel if you ate scarce amounts of candy? How would you feel if you ate a colossal pile of cherries for breakfast? How would you feel if you were given a trace amount of cereal for breakfast?

Name: _____

165. Write a Silly Story. Start by writing a simple story. Leave up to ten blanks for words to be filled in later (be sure to number the blanks). Try not to put the word *a* before a blank and try not to leave too many blanks in one sentence. On a separate sheet of paper, make a list of the kinds of words you want to fill in the blanks.

   1. A plural noun   2. An adjective   3. A past-tense verb

Have a partner offer suggestions for each type of word on your list. Write them in the correct blank. Then read your Silly Story aloud.

Name: _____

166. It's time for a dictionary scavenger hunt. Find the following in a dictionary.

1. The etymology of a word (Don't know what etymology means? Look it up! You've got a dictionary right in front of you!)

2. A word with four meanings

3. A word with seven syllables

4. Two adverbs

5. The year *astronaut* became a word

6. One thing you didn't know was in a dictionary (Hint: Look in the front and back of the book).

Name: _____

167. Write each of your current vocabulary words on an index card. Shuffle the cards and place them face down. Draw a card. Give only synonym or antonym clues to get a partner to name the word. Take turns giving clues and guessing.

Name: _____

168. What categories can you make? Sort the words below into categories—YOU decide which ones! Compare your categories with a partner.

crocodile   archaeologist   architect   caribou   gangplank

photographer   strawberry   tornado   torpedo   professional

Name: _____

169. It's time for a Word Hunt! Look through your reading and writing for compound words. Play again by searching for some of these categories of words: three-syllable words, professions, descriptive words, musical words, and location words.

Name: _____

170. Are you aware of alliteration? It's when the initial consonant or vowel sound is repeated in two or more words. Write alliterative sentences with five of your vocabulary words. Pick your favorite and make it into a bookmark.

"I'm an ignorant iguana who has no imagination and finds this task immeasurably impossible."

Word Games

Name: _____

171. Map It! Write a vocabulary word in a circle in the center of a sheet of paper. Brainstorm concepts and words related to the vocabulary word. Now, map that word like in the illustration below.

license

Ph, D.

education

6–8 years of college

college

work

school

hospital

mental health center

PSYCHOLOGIST

counsels

helping profession

advises

Word Games

Name: _____

172. On a scale of small to large, where would you rank the words? Put them in order on a scale like the one below.

puny   moderate   generous   diminutive   immense   colossal   tremendous   miniature

SMALL	LARGE

Make your own list of words and a scale. Have a partner place the words on the scale.

Word Games

Name: _____

173. Where in the world . . . ? Many words we use were borrowed from other languages. Find the country in which each of these words originated:

hurricane   lounge

bungalow   croquet

bureau   kilt

Name: _____

174. List as many compound words as you can that contain the word *house*. Next, try it with *ball*. Then see how many you can list with the word *sun*.

Name: _____

175. Concentration is a classic game. Write 10 pairs of synonyms on 20 index cards (one word on each card). Shuffle the cards and place them face down in four rows of five cards. The first player turns over two cards. If the two cards are synonyms, the player keeps the pair and play continues until no match is made. Players take turns turning over cards and matching synonyms until all cards are gone. The player with the most pairs wins. Play a variation by using 10 pairs of antonyms.

Name: _____

176. Do you like puzzles? You'll need five rectangles for this one. On the left side of each rectangle, write a vocabulary word. On the right side, write the word's definition. Then cut the rectangles apart using crooked or jagged lines. Mix up the puzzle pieces and put them in an envelope. Exchange envelopes with a partner and assemble the five puzzles.

unique — one of a kind

Word Games

Name: _____

177. Write each of your vocabulary words on an index card. The first player picks a card and draws a picture that conveys the meaning of the word. The other players try to guess the word that was drawn.

Word Games

Name: _____

178. Let's play Bingo. Everyone playing divides a card into nine squares and writes a vocabulary word on each square. Make sure that each card has the words arranged in a different order. Choose a caller to list a synonym for each word. The caller randomly calls synonyms from the list and players cover the synonyms of the words called. Play classic Bingo or cover an H shape. Does the game go too fast? Try it with sixteen-square Bingo cards.

Word Games

Name: _____

179. It's a word race! Choose a topic and set a timer for two minutes. Players write a list of words that have some connection to the topic. When time is up, players compare their lists. If any words are repeated among players, they are crossed out—only the unique words are counted. The player with the greatest number of words wins. Some topics you might use are:

space	dinner	rain	disasters
government	science	math	after-school activities

Word Games

Name: _____

180. Write each of your vocabulary words on a card. Tape a card to each player's back. Ask other players questions that will help you figure out which word is on your back.